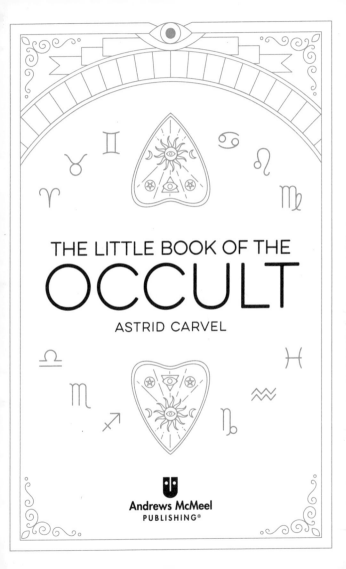

THE LITTLE BOOK OF THE
OCCULT

ASTRID CARVEL

Andrews McMeel
PUBLISHING®

THE LITTLE BOOK OF THE OCCULT

Andrews McMeel Publishing
a division of Andrews McMeel Universal
1130 Walnut Street, Kansas City, Missouri 64106

www.andrewsmcmeel.com

23 24 25 26 27 SHO 10 9 8 7 6 5 4 3 2 1

ISBN: 978-1-5248-8217-4

Library of Congress Control Number: 2022943164

Editor: Sadie Lea
Art Director/Designer: Julie Barnes
Production Editor: Brianna Westervelt
Production Manager: Chadd Keim

ATTENTION: SCHOOLS AND BUSINESSES

Andrews McMeel books are available at quantity
discounts with bulk purchase for educational, business,
or sales promotional use. For information, please
e-mail the Andrews McMeel Publishing Special Sales
Department: sales@amuniversal.com.

CONTENTS

INTRODUCTION

Welcome to *The Little Book of the Occult*. Within these pages you'll find an introduction to all things magickal. The occult refers to supernatural beliefs and practices that cannot be explained by science or religion. Occult magick offers the ability to see the future, communicate with spirits and beings beyond the material realm, and access knowledge outside of everyday human understanding.

Occult magick has a long history, stretching back to ancient times. Despite its colorful and often secretive past, occultism is thriving in the twenty-first century. You might have seen practicing witches on social media, heard about the power of manifestation from a friend, or read about the benefits of tarot for self-care.

Supernatural energy and magick are all around us, waiting for you to harness their power so you can achieve your dreams and desires. This book will guide you through the history and possibilities of the occult and introduce you to the most popular and potent forms of modern occult magick. It's also full of practical advice on how to use occult magick for self-care, achieving your goals, and creating your best life. The tips, spells, and ideas you'll find inside are all accessible and involve little or no cost to try out.

Why "magick" and not "magic"?

The extra "k" was added by prominent occultist Aleister Crowley (see page 39) to differentiate occult magick from stage magic. He considered "magick" to be anything that moves a person closer to fulfilling their destiny and favored a six-letter word over a five-letter one as he believed six to be a more potent number.

PRACTICING MAGICK SAFELY

Casting spells and using magick can be powerful, so it's important to treat these practices with respect and use your abilities wisely. Whatever energy you send out into the universe will come back to you threefold, so keep your intentions positive and do not set out to harm others.

Stick to these rules for safe occult magick:

- Respect the free will of others

- Keep your intentions positive

- Get permission before using magick on or with another person

- Protect nature and the Earth

- Practice fire safety

- Take care of your body

CHAPTER ONE

WHAT IS OCCULT MAGICK?

Occult magick is a combination of mental, mystical, and spiritual practices. Evolved through a long and rich tradition of esoteric and supernatural beliefs, the occult has long been associated with communing with ghosts and demons. While the supernatural still plays a big part, modern-day occultism focuses on connecting with our intuition, nature, and the universe for the purposes of self-care and self-discovery.

Supernatural

adjective
Anything that is attributed to a force
beyond scientific understanding
and/or the laws of nature.

OCCULT MAGICK DEFINED

Occult magick is the study, knowledge, and practice of supernatural forces. The word "occult" comes from the Latin *occulere*, which means "to hide or conceal," and it refers to the hidden nature of supernatural forces, as well as the secretive way occultism has been practiced through the ages.

This secretiveness was due to fear of religious persecution and to guard against occult power falling into the hands of those who would use it to dominate or harm others.

Today, the need to keep occult knowledge concealed has diminished, thanks to modern technology democratizing the spread of information and societies growing more liberal. Occult magick can broadly be defined as spiritual practices used to harness energies beyond those that science can explain.

WHO PRACTICES OCCULT MAGICK?

Occult magick is practiced by people from all walks of life. While it is widely practiced in its traditional settings of pagan, new age, and spiritual communities, it's also going mainstream.

Entrepreneurs like SelfishBabe app founder Olanikee Osibowale use the principles of manifestation (often called "the law of attraction") to bring wealth and success to their businesses, with amazing results.

Tarot is growing in popularity as a therapeutic tool, with practitioners like Canada-based psychologist Jayni Bloch using it to help clients access their inner selves. "Using tarot in an appropriate way can enhance therapy. It's not for fortune telling—it's a tool that gives you something to meditate on."

Occult magick is also a bona fide social media phenomenon, with a vibrant and flourishing subculture on TikTok dubbed WitchTok. Creators make content about how to use tarot cards and pendulum boards, as well as more obscure occult subjects.

WHERE DOES IT COME FROM?

For as long as humans have existed, we've tried to harness and make sense of the immense power of nature. Before we had the scientific means to study the elements, natural phenomena such as gravity, and our own bodies, people came up with supernatural and metaphysical explanations for how the world worked.

Occult magick was practiced in the ancient world, with oracles, sorcery, and witchcraft both revered and persecuted in ancient Greece. The goddesses Hecate and Circe were particularly associated with witchcraft, and depictions of occult magick have been found in ancient Roman, Mayan, and Egyptian texts.

While modern science has expanded our knowledge and understanding of the world in which we live, there are still unexplained phenomena and invisible forces that the occult practices interact with. In fact, many beliefs once thought of as supernatural are providing new breakthroughs in science, such as quantum physics and traditional herbal medicine.

WHAT DOES OCCULT MAGICK INVOLVE?

In the past, you'd need to embark on extensive training and possibly ritual initiations in order to access occult knowledge. Those who were open about their occult beliefs risked ostracism, judgment, and even imprisonment or death—especially women.

Although there are still cultures that persecute witches and followers of occult magick, it is widely accepted in most places.

Occult magick can be practiced with only the thoughts in your head and feelings in your body, and you can take your involvement as far as you feel called to. Everyone's relationship with magic is unique and personal, and yours might involve building up a knowledge of herbs, following the cycles of the moon or accessing the wisdom of your ancestors. You can practice magick alone or within a coven (see Chapter Seven), invest in tools to amplify and enhance your practice (see Chapter Four), or simply use it as part of your self-care routine. The magick is already in you, and it is yours to create.

ASK FOR WHAT YOU WANT AND BE PREPARED TO GET IT.

MAYA ANGELOU

MENTAL OCCULT MAGICK

Occult magick has evolved to encompass beliefs about the power of our thoughts. Manifestation, clairvoyance, clairsentience, the use of objects, rituals, and symbols to shift thinking patterns, letting go of limiting beliefs, and creating our lives from the inside out all play a big part in modern occult magick.

Because of this, it's perfectly possible to practice occult magick in the twenty-first century without any supernatural or metaphysical beliefs.

Psychologists recognize that negative patterns of thought are more likely to produce negative outcomes. Therefore, training your mind to believe certain positive ideas makes those positive outcomes more likely to find their way into your life—this is manifestation in a nutshell (see page 90 for more).

For example, if you think about how unpopular you are, you're more likely to notice people being unfriendly to you. If you think about having a new friend and believe you're meant to have one, you're more likely to spot a potential new friend when they come your way.

There's still a measure of belief required, but it's not as big of a leap as it can initially seem.

METAPHYSICAL OCCULT MAGICK

Metaphysics comes from the Greek *meta ta physika*—"after the physics of nature." It means ideas and phenomena that fall outside of human sensory perception—so anything that someone believes to exist but can't be seen, smelled, heard, touched, or tasted.

Concepts like time, love, and existence can be described as metaphysical, and occult magick seeks to understand and gain influence over the metaphysical world using magickal processes. Energy, spirits, and souls are also metaphysical concepts and can be accessed using extrasensory perception (ESP), as a means to gain insight into other energetic realms.

SPIRITUAL OCCULT MAGICK

The spiritual side of occult magick relates to a belief in something bigger than ourselves. Some call this god, goddess, energy, the universe, source, or even simply, creativity.

The beauty of the occult is that it is not strict about beliefs—you are free to use the words, concepts, and images in your magickal practice that feel comfortable, useful, and powerful to you.

If you're interested in dabbling with occult magick, it's useful to spend some time thinking about how you think about yourself spiritually—and how you are connected to the rest of humanity and the universe. Some love the idea that we are all made of stardust—and therefore connected via the energy of the Big Bang—while the more traditional concept of a soul resonates with others.

Get comfortable relating to yourself as a spiritual being with powers of perception beyond your five senses. It's the key to accessing your magick.

YOU'VE ALWAYS HAD THE POWER, MY DEAR. YOU JUST HAD TO LEARN IT FOR YOURSELF.

L. FRANK BAUM

CHAPTER TWO

WHY PRACTICE OCCULT MAGICK?

There are many compelling reasons to begin practicing occult magick. You never know just how powerful you are until you tap into your hidden depths. Depending on your intentions for practicing, magick can bring you luck, wealth, love, opportunities, improve your outlook, and ultimately enrich your life.

ABUNDANCE

Abundance is the state of having plenty of everything you need. Many of us are stuck in scarcity—that is, a lack of the things we need and an instinct to compete and hoard our resources—modern life can have this effect on us.

Practicing occult magick involves shifting your mindset toward the belief that there is an abundance of money, love, time, and opportunity in the universe—enough for everybody. Using occult practices such as spell casting, manifestation, and the intuitive arts will connect you to a new outlook on life and allow you to relax in the knowledge that you are able to call whatever inspiration, accomplishment, or opportunity that you wish for into your life.

POSITIVITY

Applying the principles of occult magick to your life has a profound effect on the way you think. Understanding that you are a co-creator of your life—that you have power and agency to choose your own path rather than life being something that happens to you—brings with it a sense of peace and positivity.

Intuitive practices such as tarot and scrying help reframe negative thought patterns and allow you to tap into an inner wisdom that's not easily accessed using non-magickal methods.

While some tarot cards may seem foreboding on the surface, you'll come to learn that each card—and every human experience—contains both light and dark. For example, the Death card looks ominous at first, but dive deeper into the imagery and you'll discover that it signifies endings, which go hand in hand with new beginnings.

MINDFULNESS

Mindfulness is the practice of paying your full attention to the present moment, and all magick requires you to be fully present in your practice. Your attention is the single most powerful magickal tool in your possession and a mindful approach is key to wielding it effectively.

Whether you're communicating with spirits, reading tarot cards, or casting spells, a state of mindful awareness is essential to getting the most out of occult magick.

The health benefits of mindfulness are well documented—it's been found to improve emotional regulation and focus, as well as reduce stress, anxiety, and rumination. As a discipline, the aim of mindfulness is to gain greater control over your thoughts and reduce mental "chatter," bringing you a greater sense of peace and stillness. Occult wisdom says that the more we are able to control our thoughts, the stronger our connection to our power becomes. Using occult magick as a mindfulness practice will increase both your emotional well-being and your magickal abilities.

BELIEF

Research shows that believing in something bigger than yourself—whether organized religion, spirituality, or magick—has proven mental health benefits. It's been found to lead to increased resilience and contentment with life. These benefits are thought to be down to the ability this type of belief gives you to trust in an unseen order and see logic in a world that can often feel chaotic.

Occult magick allows you to tap into the unseen, mysterious forces that are at play in our lives. Occult wisdom tells us to trust in the mystery of the universe and to recognize that we are all connected to its power and energy.

KNOWLEDGE

The occult has a rich and fascinating history—we'll delve into it in the next chapter—and it also contains diverse and complex philosophies. In short, dipping your toe into the occult will open the door to a huge new source of knowledge.

The occult is a broad collection of belief systems and practices, and the path you take is up to you. One of the most attractive things about occult magick is the freedom to create your own interpretations and beliefs—everyone's relationship to the occult is completely unique.

As fascinating as the history and culture of the occult is, you'll also gain a huge amount of self-knowledge from connecting with the subject. Part of creating a practice is learning about your own mind and your relationship to symbols, rituals, and ideas.

CONNECTION

Occult magick is fun and sociable—getting involved, even in a small way, will attract like-minded people into your life—that's part of the magic.

Wherever you are, there's bound to be a community of people interested in the occult. Numbers are hard to ascertain, but it's clear that the number of practicing witches and occultists has exploded in recent decades. The most recent statistics found more than 65,000 Wiccan and pagan people in the UK, and about 1.5 million in the US—but figures are thought to be higher thanks to social media.

Witchcraft and the occult are huge online. WitchTok and esoteric Instagram accounts such as @TheHoodWitch and @Witches.of.insta offer accessible, bite-sized content and a way to connect with the online occult community.

WHAT I NEEDED WAS COURAGE, AND IT WAS GRANTED TO ME THROUGH THE SPIRITUAL WORLD, WHICH BESTOWED RARE AND WONDERFUL INSTRUCTION.

HILMA AF KLINT

CHAPTER THREE

A BRIEF HISTORY OF OCCULT PRACTICES AND ANCIENT MAGIC MYTH-BUSTING

The history of the occult is varied and fascinating. In this chapter we'll explore its origins and development through the ages, while meeting some of the occult's key characters.

It's worth noting that there are still cultures and regions in the world—such as Ghana and Saudi Arabia—where practicing witchcraft is punishable by death. This book focuses on witchcraft in the West. To learn more, there are further resources on page 126.

ORIGINS

Humans have worshipped, feared, and practiced magick since before recorded history. Forms of divination and a belief in supernatural forces or beings have been found in every society across the globe.

Western occultism as we know it today originated from a secret ancient philosophy, a combination of ancient Greek magic, astrology, alchemy, and Jewish mysticism.

Jewish mysticism or *Kabbalah* is an esoteric and mystical philosophy, originating in the first century. Broadly speaking, it deals with the ways in which followers can become one with the divine through ritual practices.

In ancient Greece, occult magick was part of everyday life, and there was little distinction between science, medicine, and magick. The Greek word *pharmakeia*—meaning "magic potions"—is the root of our modern term "pharmaceutical." Ordinary citizens would visit practitioners to help with their problems, and rulers would use magick to protect their kingdoms. There are records of the death penalty being issued for the use of harmful magick, and philosophers such as Plato campaigned for magick to be outlawed because they believed power belonged to rulers rather than ordinary people.

HECATE, GODDESS OF WITCHCRAFT

Hecate was the ancient Greek goddess of witchcraft, crossroads, and the moon. Shrines to Hecate, who is often represented as a triple goddess, would be placed over doorways to homes, temples, and cities in order to protect them from restless spirits.

Call on Hecate by including yew or garlic in your magick and by lighting torches.

MIDDLE AGES AND EARLY MODERN PERIOD

During the Middle Ages in Europe, belief in magick and the occult was widespread, and local wise women were whom most ordinary people turned to for both healthcare and magickal assistance.

While Christianity was the dominant religion, pagan beliefs—in things like fairies and elves—were still common, as were pagan monuments and burial sites. Even Christians believed that pagan spirits existed and had the ability to grant powers to humans.

As European scholars and leaders began to learn about the power of occult magick through communication with other cultures, they feared that it would challenge the power of the Christian church. To combat this threat, they constructed the myth that these wise women and folk healers were in league with the devil, in order to create fear and distrust for practitioners of magick. Labeled as witches, thousands of people—around 84 percent of them women— were executed between the sixteenth and eighteenth centuries.

Witches became scapegoats for any and all bad luck, misfortune, or disaster, including the bubonic plague, bad harvests, and minor diseases. "Proof" that someone was a witch could be anything from a wart or birthmark to being too rich or too poor, too forthright or too strange.

King James I of England was convinced that a coven of witches summoned a storm to drown him. His obsession with witchcraft led him to write a book on the subject, *Daemonologie*, and make witchcraft punishable by death in 1604. During James I's reign, William Shakespeare exploited this popular fear of witchcraft, famously opening *Macbeth* with the scene of three witches plotting against a king.

The most well-known witch trials occurred in Salem, Massachusetts, but other notorious trials happened in Pendle, England; Berwick, Scotland; Valais, France; and Trier, Germany.

The centuries-long craze for witch-hunting stigmatized the practice of occult magick, driving it underground for hundreds of years.

In 2022, First Minister of Scotland Nicola Sturgeon officially pardoned and apologized to "all those who were accused, convicted, vilified, or executed under the Witchcraft Act of 1563." Similar campaigns around the world are calling for witches to be pardoned and their lives commemorated.

ANNA GÖLDI, EUROPE'S LAST "WITCH"

Göldi was the last person in Europe to be executed as a witch.

In Switzerland in 1765, 31-year-old Anna Göldi was forced to flee her hometown when her baby died shortly after birth. She took work as a servant in the home of a wealthy physician, Johann Jakob Tschudi, in the nearby town of Glarus.

Several years later, in 1782, needles were found in Tschudi's daughter's milk. Göldi was fired and weeks later—despite no longer living at the residence—she was accused of causing another of his daughters to vomit metallic objects. She was arrested for witchcraft, tortured until she confessed, and was beheaded in June 1782.

Historians have found that Göldi was having an affair with Tschudi when she was fired, and the witchcraft accusations came after she threatened to reveal their relationship.

Two hundred years after her death, Swiss journalist and lawyer Walter Hauser secured a pardon from the local government in Glarus and went on to found the Anna Göldi museum.

THE EIGHTEENTH CENTURY AND THE WITCHCRAFT ACT

In the early years of the eighteenth century, the craze for witchcraft was dying down across the Western world, and in 1735 the Witchcraft Act was passed, making it illegal to accuse people of witchcraft and ending the practice of trial and execution of witches.

While playing cards had been used for both games and divination since the fifteenth century, the first tarot deck for occult purposes was published in 1789 by Jean-Baptiste Alliette under his pseudonym Etteilla. Alliette had been taught to read the tarot in Paris by northern Italian occultists at the Société Apollinienne, a scholarly club founded by Antoine Court de Gébelin.

The popularity of tarot grew thanks to its association with Egyptian wisdom and symbolism. Egyptian philosophy was popular among Parisian society in the eighteenth century, and the theory that the tarot contains the wisdom of ancient Egypt was spread by Alliette and Court de Gébelin.

FRANZ MESMER AND THE BIRTH OF HYPNOSIS

Franz Mesmer (1734–1815) was a German physician who came up with the theory of "animal magnetism"— the idea that natural energy could be transferred between everything in the universe. His theory gave way to the practice of hypnosis or mesmerism.

Demonstrations of mesmerism were hugely popular in nineteenth-century Europe. At these demonstrations people would be put in a trance, in which their bodies would convulse and they would be under the control of the practitioner. While in a trance, it was believed that people could communicate with spirits and enter visionary states.

THE NINETEENTH CENTURY AND SPIRITUALISM

The occult went mainstream in the nineteenth century, through a particular fascination with mediumship that was sweeping the English-speaking world. As science was advancing more rapidly, including the discovery of electricity and Darwin's theory of evolution, the possibility of invisible forces at play in the everyday lives of human beings became hugely interesting to many people.

Séances and displays of mediumship were popular among the upper and middle classes, and it was believed that the spirits of the dead could be contacted and communicated with using occult tools and rituals. Often named "spiritualism," followers believed that these spirits had the ability to achieve greater wisdom and higher states of consciousness than the living, and could therefore impart advice and guidance during séances.

Especially popular among women, spiritualists would meet in each other's homes and perform séances or in halls for trance lectures. Successful mediums were also overwhelmingly female—because women were thought to be more sensitive and therefore more able to tune into subtle energies.

The spiritualist movement began in 1848 in Hydesville, New York. Two teenage sisters—Maggie and Kate Fox—claimed that they were in communication with a murdered former resident of their home. With the help of a group of radical Quakers, the sisters quickly grew famous, delighting audiences in New York and throughout the US.

The spectacle of mediumship caught on and spread across the English-speaking world. Mediums and spiritualism are still popular, with spiritualist churches and practitioners in most towns and cities across the West.

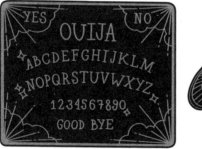

HELENA BLAVATSKY AND EASTERN PHILOSOPHIES IN THE WEST

Born in 1831 in modern-day Ukraine, Helena Blavatsky traveled Europe with her aristocratic family as a child and developed an interest in the occult as a teenager. Her quest for knowledge took her all over the world, and she moved to the US in the 1870s, founding the Theosophical Society alongside Henry Steel Olcott in 1875. Her vision was of a bringing together of science, religion, and philosophy with ancient occult wisdom. A controversial figure during her lifetime, she was heralded as a visionary by her supporters and derided as a fake by her critics. Her work and ideas are credited with spreading Eastern philosophy in the West, as well as inspiring later Western occult and esoteric movements.

PAMELA COLMAN SMITH, THE TAROT ARTIST

Born in London in 1878, Pamela "Pixie" Colman Smith is the artist behind the most widely used and recognized tarot deck today. With publisher Rider and poet Arthur Edward Waite, the Smith-Rider-Waite tarot deck was first published in 1909 featuring 78 of Colman Smith's illustrations.

During her lifetime, Colman Smith received little recognition or financial success. She died in Bude, Cornwall, UK, in 1951.

In 1971 the rights to the Smith-Rider-Waite tarot deck were bought by US Games, and the deck became hugely successful. Today, millions of copies have been sold all over the world, and Colman Smith's illustrations have inspired countless artists.

LEARN FROM EVERYTHING, SEE EVERYTHING, AND ABOVE ALL FEEL EVERYTHING! FIND EYES WITHIN, LOOK FOR THE DOOR INTO THE UNKNOWN COUNTRY.

PAMELA COLMAN SMITH

THE TWENTIETH CENTURY AND THE RISE OF THE OCCULT

Throughout the twentieth century, belief in the occult spread. As the authority of the Christian church and the rigidity of the class system decreased in the West, a willingness to embrace new ideas about magic, energy, and the universe grew.

Abstract art was born in the twentieth century, when creatives began to look beyond the traditional rules of art. A connection with spirits and higher beings was a feature of the creative practice of abstract painters such as Hilma af Klint and Wassily Kandinsky, and poets like W. B. Yeats. Another developing discipline was that of psychology with Swiss psychiatrist Carl Jung a prominent new thinker. Jung was a believer in spirits and the afterlife and developed a theory of "the collective unconscious" and synchronicity in psychotherapy.

During the 1960s the hippie movement brought about a resurgence in the occult, with Wicca, witchcraft, and pagan practices at the cutting edge of a new culture. The occult reached television and cinema audiences, with shows like *The Addams Family* and *Bewitched*, and films such as *Rosemary's Baby* entertaining millions of viewers.

ALEISTER CROWLEY, THE PROPHET

Occultist, magician, poet, painter, novelist, and mountaineer Aleister Crowley was born in 1875 in Leamington Spa, Warwickshire, UK. He trained in ceremonial magic with the Hermetic Order of the Golden Dawn. During a holiday to Cairo with his wife, Rose, in 1904, Crowley began hearing a disembodied voice—that of a spiritual messenger named Aiwass. Aiwass dictated a book to Crowley, entitled *The Book of the Law*, which claimed Crowley was a prophet for a new era. In 1907 he used this text to found a new occult philosophy named Thelema and a new esoteric organization called A∴A∴ .

Crowley went on to write several more books and publish the *Thoth* tarot deck. Crowley was a pioneer of sex magick and experimented with hallucinogenic drugs to communicate with other realms. In his later life, he battled a heroin addiction and is rumored to have worked as a spy for the British government in the Second World War. He died in Hastings, East Sussex, UK, in 1947.

THE NEW AGE

From the 1970s onward, occultism evolved into what became known as the "New Age" movement. An interest in both the occult practices of the nineteenth and early twentieth centuries, alongside belief in aliens and UFOs, meant the movement was home to a huge diversity of beliefs and practices.

Alternatives to Western medicine, as well as a focus on the spirituality of the individual, characterized this new version of occultism. Occult and esoteric practices such as astrology, energy healing, and transcendental meditation came to prominence, with horoscopes appearing regularly in major newspapers and the benefits of meditation being promoted in the West.

New Age spirituality had strong ties to left-wing progressive countercultures, but a similar interest in the power of the occult also grew on the political right during the twentieth century and continues today.

ROSALEEN NORTON, THE BRAVE WITCH

Born in 1917, Rosaleen Norton was an Australian artist and witch. She lived in Kings Cross, Sydney, where she led a coven of witches, worshipped the god Pan, and practiced magick. Norton said she was born a witch, and as a child she chose to sleep not in the family home but in a tent in the garden with her pet spider, Horatius, guarding the entrance.

As an adult she became an occult artist, painting murals of goblins, vampires, witches, and ghosts. In 1955 she was accused of leading Satanist black masses, which she denied. The tabloid press stirred up public outcry about her and her work, making her into a local celebrity and tourist attraction.

Norton asserted that she was not a Satanist, but a pagan witch, and continued to explain her beliefs to those who sought her out. She died in 1979 and is quoted as saying, "I came into the world bravely; I'll go out bravely."

THE TWENTY-FIRST CENTURY AND TECH-LED OCCULTISM

The growth of the internet and social media in the twenty-first century has made the occult available to anyone with a Wi-Fi connection and an interest in the mysteries of the universe. Not only have the ancient and traditional occult beliefs and practices been popularized, but they've also evolved to embrace and integrate technology.

Mystics like Gabriella Abrão and Bri Luna use platforms such as Instagram to examine the nature of reality, cast spells, and spread occult knowledge to their followers. In the hands of a twenty-first-century witch, a smartphone becomes a portal, and occult practices are centered around self-care and emotional healing.

SPELLS ARE EQUAL PARTS MAGIC AND EQUAL PARTS A TRICK OF THE BRAIN, A GAME WITH THE SUBCONSCIOUS.

GABRIELLA ABRÃO

CHAPTER FOUR

TOOLS FOR OCCULT MAGICK

While magick lives inside you, using magickal tools and objects will amplify and channel your intentions, allowing you to experiment with your power and diversify your practice. In this chapter you'll find some of the most common and powerful tools for practicing occult magick. There's information on each tool, a look at how to use it, and a guide to sourcing your own.

HERBS

Herbs have been used in spell casting and occult rituals for millennia. Herbs, plants, and scents are a powerful way to intensify a spell and amplify a ritual. Because of their medicinal properties, they've long been used for healing the body and have rich symbolism and supernatural associations.

You can use fresh or dried plants and herbs, incense, or essential oils, which are all widely available online and in supermarkets.

Different herbs are associated with different properties:

- **Acacia**—for clairvoyance
- **Angelica**—for protection
- **Basil**—for money and fertility
- **Bay**—for lifting a curse
- **Catnip**—for love, happiness, friendship, and courage
- **Cedar**—to heal a fraught mind
- **Chamomile**—for a change of luck, circumstance, or prosperity

- **Cherry**—for love and friendship
- **Chive**—for banishing negativity
- **Cinnamon**—to attract money
- **Clove**—to stop negative words being said about you
- **Comfrey**—for safe travel and protection
- **Dill**—to protect new life
- **Fern**—to encourage rainfall
- **Frankincense**—for good luck
- **Garlic**—for protection and dispelling negativity
- **Lavender**—for good sleep and to attract new love
- **Mint**—for healing and protection
- **Patchouli**—for fertility
- **Pine**—for exorcism and to return negative vibes to their senders
- **Rosemary**—for memory, protection, and finding spells
- **Sage**—to cleanse bad energy and for repulsion spells
- **Thyme**—for good health and healing
- **Vetivert**—for protection against thieves and black magic
- **Willow**—to attract love
- **Wisteria**—for protection
- **Ylang-ylang**—add potency to love and healing spells

CANDLES

Candles are a relatively modern addition to spell casting because it was not until the twentieth century that they became affordable and easy to come by. The modern witch often casts their spells by candlelight, as the flame provides a focus for their energies and desires. Different colored candles are used for different intentions:

- **Blue**—protection from evil spirits, healing

- **Gold**—wealth and success

- **Green**—money, luck, curing illness, growth

- **Red**—luck, love and romance, prosperity and healing

- **Silver**—fertility, success

- **White**—new beginnings, creativity

Choose your candle depending on the spell or ritual you're using it for. If your spell requires your candle to burn all the way down, a smaller candle is best. Likewise, some spells need a seven-day candle or a particular shape.

Candles can be dressed with oil, herbs, and plants. Online, you'll find spell candles with crystals embedded in their wax, and simple beeswax spell candles are widely and cheaply available.

Candles are also used for divination and scrying. Seek wisdom in the movements of the flame, or pour candle wax into a bowl of cold water to read the shapes it forms.

CRYSTALS

Crystals hold huge magickal potential. Alive with magickal natural energy, they're used in electrical products due to their conductivity, which makes them the ultimate power source when casting spells. Each stone possesses different energies and properties. Here are some of the most potent:

▷ AMETHYST

Place one of these purple crystals by your bed to aid sleep, particularly if you are feeling anxious.

▷ AQUAMARINE

This ice-blue stone symbolizes hope and good fortune.

▷ CARNELIAN

This fiery orange stone revives, restores, and cuts negative ties.

⬦ CELESTINE

Opens channels with heavenly beings and spirit guides.

⬦ CITRINE

Promotes motivation, activates creativity, and encourages self-expression.

⬦ JADE

Symbolizes longevity, knowledge, and strength.

⬦ QUARTZ

Aids healing of both physical and emotional imbalances.

⬦ ROSE QUARTZ

The crystal of love, it also calms emotional turmoil.

⬦ TIGER'S EYE

Used for seeing into the future and finding solutions.

⬦ TOURMALINE

Repels negative energy.

TAROT CARDS

Tarot cards are a popular way to practice twenty-first-century occult magick. Originally produced for gambling and card games, tarot became popular as a divination tool in eighteenth-century France, with readers using the cards to predict the future and communicate with spirits.

A tarot deck is made up of four suits—most often swords, wands, pentacles, and cups. Each suit is composed of an ace, the numbers 2–10, and four court cards—page, knight, queen, and king. These suited cards are known as the minor arcana. In addition to the 56 suited cards, the major arcana contains 22 individual archetype cards.

Today, tarot is used to bring clarity to a confusing situation, guidance for tricky decisions, and as a tool for self-care and self-reflection. Modern tarot artists have created myriad new interpretations of these traditional cards, breathing new life into the tarot and bringing it to a new audience. Turn to page 81 for more on using the tarot in your practice.

A common misconception about first tarot decks is that you shouldn't buy them. The theory goes that your first deck should be a gift from someone who loves you, so it brings with it the energy of love and effortlessness.

If you're lucky enough to be gifted a tarot deck, congratulations—that deck will serve you well. If, on the other hand, you don't want to wait, you can buy your own and infuse your purchase with that same loving, intentional energy.

Browse specialist stores and websites to see which decks are out there. You might like to consider a price range before you start looking—the right deck at the right price will find you.

You'll come across both tarot and oracle decks in your search. There are differences, but both can be used for divination, manifestation, and self-care.

Make sure you're calm and centered, and pay attention to which decks you're drawn to. Use your intuition to guide you to the deck that's meant for you.

EACH IDEA SPOKEN TURNS INTO A SPELL WE CAST, ON OURSELVES AND THOSE AROUND US.

DON MIGUEL RUIZ

OUIJA BOARD

"Ouija: The Wonderful Talking Board" first went on sale in 1891. Featuring the letters of the alphabet, the numbers 0–9, plus the words "yes," "no," "hello," and "goodbye," the Ouija board enables spirits and the living to communicate with each other.

Using a planchette—a teardrop-shaped device with a window and sometimes wheels—mediums place their hands on the planchette and allow any spirits present to move their hand, spelling out messages on the board.

Invented as a way of making communication with the dead more efficient, it put an end to mediums calling out the letters of the alphabet and waiting for a sign at the appropriate letter. The Ouija board made contacting other realms almost as simple as using the latest in Earth-bound technology—the telephone.

The board was named "Ouija" through mediumship—it named itself and told the manufacturers at Kennard Novelty Company that "Ouija" meant "good luck." The board was granted a patent after Helen Peters—the sister-in-law of one of the company's founders—successfully used the board to guess the patent officer's name.

Ouija boards can be bought cheaply online or in specialist shops. As the boards are simply a method for streamlining communication between realms, you can also make your own.

Take a large piece of cardstock, wood, or plastic and write on it all the letters, numbers, and words from the classic Ouija board design.

Use an upturned glass in place of a planchette and allow the spirits to guide you.

TOOLS FOR SCRYING

Scrying can be found in multiple cultures, and while the term "scrying" is from the Old English meaning "to reveal," the practice did not originate in England. One of the earliest documented forms of scrying took place in 3000 BC, in China, where glossy egg yolks were used.

Scrying is the act of gazing at a suitable medium and entering a trance-like state in order to receive guidance or messages. Reflective surfaces such as water, a crystal ball, or a dark mirror are excellent for scrying, as well as fire, wax, and smoke.

Like other forms of divination, scrying involves a connection between human intuition and supernatural energies. Scrying reveals images, shapes, or messages that the reader interprets using their wisdom and knowledge. Turn to page 105 for a closer look at practicing scrying.

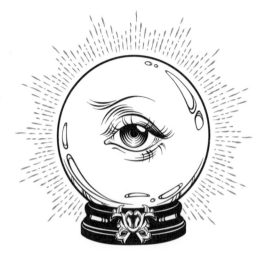

Crystal balls can be bought in specialist shops and online, as can obsidian scrying mirrors. But you probably have perfectly good scrying mediums in your home already. Candles can be used for fire, wax, and smoke scrying, a plain-colored bowl filled with water is all you need for water scrying, and your smartphone, when turned off, is a powerful dark mirror.

BOOK OF SHADOWS

This is the place where a witch records their rituals and spells, like a witchy recipe book. It's helpful to keep a record of when you performed a spell, the ingredients used, perhaps how you were feeling at the time, the moon's phase, and the outcome. It means you can look back on your spells, see what has worked and what hasn't, and perhaps consider ways of tweaking them if you want to perform them again. The term "book of shadows" was coined by Gerald Gardner, the founder of modern Wicca, as he recommended that the book be kept hidden—in the shadows—and private. The traditions of witches and their practices have been kept alive by these books.

Your own book of shadows can be as basic or elaborate as you wish—a simple notebook will suffice or a ring binder for ease of organizing your pages. Most importantly, the front page must have your name on it somewhere, as this will bind the wisdom within your book of shadows to you and infuse it with your energy.

Your book of shadows can be personalized in all manner of ways, such as scenting the pages with your favorite oils or perhaps decorating the cover with images from magazines or the internet that speak to you in magickal ways. Many twenty-first-century witches choose to document their practices on a computer—but make sure you back it up! You could have a dedicated USB stick to store your book of shadows and create a special pouch for it out of fabric.

WAND

The use of wands for magickal purposes dates back to the Middle Kingdom of Egypt—around 2000 BC. Hippopotamus tusks were carved into wands and used during childbirth to invoke Taweret, the hippopotamus goddess of childbirth. Later, Egyptian wands would have inscriptions of spells and intentions of the bearer. Wands were also used in Greek mythology by the gods Hermes, Athena, and Circe.

Wands have been used in the occult arts since around the thirteenth century. The Latin grimoire *Oathbound Book of Honorius* included the use of wands, as well as the sixteenth-century *Key of*

Solomon, which was used by occultists for hundreds of years.

Wands are also a suit in the tarot, representing the element of fire, growth, creativity, and energy.

Wands are often used as a tool for practical magick by the modern-day witch. They are a way of directing the magick into a particular place and building up energy during a spell. You don't need to spend money on a wand—a twig will suffice, but you can't just snap it off the nearest tree; you must ask for the blessings of the woods before you take it. Never use green wood, as this is likely to crack. Green wood contains sap—you want a twig that has been dried out. The best wood is that which has fallen from the tree and been left to dry on the ground. Hazel is traditionally used for wands as it symbolizes fairness, equality, and wisdom. Other woods you can use include driftwood that has been smoothed by the waves and still contains the energy of the sea.

You can personalize your wand by painting or drawing witchcraft symbols on it (see Chapter 5), or if a crystal or found object has a particular resonance for you—such as a piece of sea glass or perhaps a scrap of fabric from a much-loved item—you can add it to the tip of the wand.

PENDULUM

A pendulum is an object suspended on a length of string or chain held in the hand and allowed to sway freely in order to communicate a message. Pendulums are most useful for obtaining "yes" or "no" answers, but with the use of what is known as a pendulum board or cloth, they can be used to divine more complex responses.

Pendulums have long been used to predict the sex of an unborn baby, by allowing it to swing above an expectant mother's belly. Much like a planchette and Ouija board, a pendulum requires you to relax and let it move of its own accord, while interpreting its movements.

A pendulum can be made from any weighty object suspended from a flexible string or chain. Rings, keys, and pendants make perfect pendulums, or you can buy crystal pendulums from specialist stores.

For "yes" or "no" questions, no extra tools are required. If you'd like to use a pendulum for more detailed communication, you can make or buy a cloth or board. Include whichever words, images, and symbols are most useful to you—some pendulum cloths have the letters of the alphabet, while others show the chakras, the phases of the moon, or the signs of the zodiac.

DOWSING RODS

A dowsing rod is a Y-shaped piece of hazel, rowan, or willow, or a pair of L-shaped pieces of metal. These rods have been used throughout history to search for underground water, minerals, treasure, and even dead bodies.

In occult practices, dowsing rods are used to pick up energetic vibrations and the presence of ghosts and spirits—the rods will move when they detect energetic activity. In the twentieth century, the Earth mysteries movement popularized the theory that straight energetic tracks, known as "ley lines," exist between historic landmarks and serve as magnets for supernatural activity.

Dowsing rods are often used for cleansing a space or releasing trapped spirits, as the rods can lead the bearer to the specific point in a room or building where negative energy is strongest.

Metal dowsing rods can be bought online or at specialist stores. If you live near a forest, look for forked sticks from hazel, rowan, or willow trees. You can also use your pendulum for dowsing, as it can pick up energy in the same way.

If you decide to find wood for your dowsing rods, do so with intention. Look for forked branches that have fallen and dried on the ground, as these will be sturdy and rigid. Consider leaving something of your own as an offering of gratitude to the forest, like a scrap of fabric, a small stone, or sprig of herbs.

You can use a knife to carefully inscribe your wooden dowsing rods with a symbol or intention—perhaps for clarity or success—to amplify and focus its energy.

THE WORLD IS FULL OF MAGIC THINGS, PATIENTLY WAITING FOR OUR SENSES TO GROW SHARPER.

W. B. YEATS

CHAPTER FIVE

SIGNS AND SYMBOLS OF OCCULT MAGICK

Symbols are very important in the occult.
Used to invoke spirits, set intentions,
and strengthen magick, getting familiar
with occult symbolism will help deepen
your relationship with your practice.
This chapter contains some of the most
powerful signs and symbols of the occult.

PENTACLE

The pentacle (or pentagram) is a five-point star encased in a circle. It's an important symbol in the occult and is considered a potent protection against evil forces. The symbol itself, whether enclosed in a circle or on its own, dates back to the Babylonian empire around 600 BC and possibly earlier. It was used by early Christians to represent Jesus's five wounds.

In Wicca and occult wisdom, each point represents an element: earth, air, fire, and water, with the fifth element, the top point, signifying the spirit. The circle around the star represents eternity, the cycle of life, and nature, and also acts as a protective field.

The Lesser Banishing Ritual of the Pentagram is a ceremonial magick ritual in the occult and is used to cleanse a space in preparation for performing magick. Turn to page 122 for more on this ritual.

INVERTED PENTACLE

When the pentacle symbol is inverted, it has an altogether darker meaning. The upside-down pentacle was first used in the nineteenth century by French occultist Éliphas Lévi to denote evil. It's especially associated with Satan and Satanism because it's shaped like the horned half-goat, half-human figure Baphomet, who represents the devil.

In *The Secret Doctrine*, Helena Blavatsky claimed the inverted pentacle represents the current age of materialism. In the twenty-first century, the inverted pentacle is most associated with the Church of Satan. Although the Christian church has accused occultists and folk healers of devil worship throughout history, modern Satanism is not a magickal or supernatural organization. Founded in the 1960s by Anton LaVey, Satanists are atheists and libertarians who largely reject occult and spiritual beliefs.

THE FOUR ELEMENTS

In occult magick, each of the four elements has its own energy and associations. The symbols represent not just the physical elements but also their properties and power:

EARTH

An upside-down equilateral triangle with a horizontal line, earth represents the material world, belongings, and the body. It corresponds with the pentacles suit in the tarot.

AIR

An equilateral triangle with a horizontal line across it, air governs knowledge, action, and change. It is the element of the swords suit in the tarot.

FIRE

An equilateral triangle symbolizing both destruction and creation, fire represents passion, energy, and sexuality. The wands suit in the tarot is governed by the element of fire.

WATER

An inverted equilateral triangle, water is the symbol of emotion, intuition, and cleansing. It is the element of the cups suit in tarot.

ANCIENT EGYPTIAN SYMBOLS

ANKH

This symbol, which looks like a cross with a loop at the top, is the ancient Egyptian symbol for eternal life. It is used in protection spells and to ward off danger.

EYE OF HORUS

The eye of Horus is the ancient Egyptian symbol used to ward off the evil eye. The symbol was painted on fishermen's boats to protect them from evil curses while at sea; it was also found on coffins to protect the dead in the afterlife. The symbol can be used around the home or worn as a talisman to guard against jealous or malignant energies.

HORNED GOD

A circle with a pair of horns on top is the Wiccan symbol for masculine deities of nature, such as Herne. In occult magick, the horned god is associated with the ancient Egyptian deity Osiris, the inverted pentacle, and the Devil card in the tarot.

TRIPLE GODDESS

This is a full moon with two crescents—one appearing before the full moon to represent the waxing moon, and the other after the full moon to represent the waning moon. This symbol is also associated with womanhood and is used in empowerment spells and for harnessing the moon's power. In occult magick, the triple goddess symbol is associated with the Greek goddess Hecate and with the potential phases of a woman's life—maiden, mother, and crone.

SIGILS

A sigil is a symbol used to represent a spirit or a desired outcome. The word comes from the Latin *sigillum*, meaning "seal," which is the root of many other English words such as "signature," "sign," and "signal."

In medieval magick, sigils were used to summon demons, with each occult entity having its own sigil. These sigils were created using a complex system of numbers and shapes and were believed to harness the power of the spirits they invoked. These would be used to repel evil, bring good luck, or produce a desired outcome.

In modern occult magick, sigils are used to create powerful symbols that enhance intentions, bring protection, and supercharge manifestation.

USING SIGILS FOR MANIFESTATION

There are many different types of sigils, and many methods to make them, including using complex charts, astrology, and even musical notes. One of the simplest ways to create a sigil is the word method. Here's how it's done:

First, write your intention in capital letters in the present tense. Make it as brief, clear, and to the point as you can. For example:

I AM SAFE AND CALM

Next, eliminate any vowels, gaps, and repeated letters:

✦ **MSFNDCL**

Take your remaining letters and combine them to make a symbol. You can play around with the letters' proportions or use only parts of them—your sigil doesn't need to be decipherable, it only needs to contain the energy of your intention, so let your intuition guide you.

Once you have your sigil, you can use it to manifest your intention. Draw it on your body, on candles, in your grimoire or journal, and on objects relevant to your intention. Sigils also make a great addition to your manifestation practice (see page 90).

ART IS, LIKE MAGIC,
THE SCIENCE OF
MANIPULATING SYMBOLS,
WORDS, OR IMAGES TO
ACHIEVE CHANGES IN
CONSCIOUSNESS.

ALAN MOORE

THE PHILOSOPHER'S STONE

This symbol represents perfection and immortality and was a central symbol of mystic alchemists, searching for the mythic alchemical substance of the same name that can turn base metals into silver and gold. While the practice of alchemy died out many years ago, the symbol is still used to represent enlightenment, transformation, and bliss.

ABRACADABRA

Although you may know it from children's entertainers, abracadabra is a magickal formula with a long occult history. The first known mention of the word is in the second-century Roman book *Liber Medicinalis*, advising malaria sufferers to wear an amulet bearing the formula. It has been used in many cultures to ward off serious disease and invoke protection.

It's also used to enhance manifestation, as it translates from the ancient Aramaic to "I create as I speak." Use the word and symbol to strengthen and amplify your words.

CHAPTER SIX

PRACTICING OCCULT MAGICK

Many of the occult magick practices mentioned so far in this book have fallen out of favor—much like alchemy, demon summoning, and mesmerism. The occult of the twenty-first century centers on the practices that strengthen intuition and bring abundance and healing. In this chapter you'll be introduced to some of the most popular occult magick around today—tarot, manifestation, divination, spell casting, and communication with spirits. Occult magick is powerful, so it's best to treat it with respect and expect success.

Occult magick can work in unexpected ways, so it's important to be open, patient, and flexible with your expectations. Sometimes it may seem like a spell hasn't worked or has backfired—trust the process and remember that what's for you will find you.

CREATING AN ALTAR

An altar is any space in your home that is dedicated to your magick. Your altar can be a windowsill, shelf, table, or corner—size doesn't matter, it's the energy that counts. Follow your intuition to choose a location for your altar in your home—it can be an entire room or just a small space. Your altar is where you go to practice magick.

Furnish your altar with whichever images and objects nourish your magickal practice—things like crystals, inspiring photos, written intentions, incense, and tarot cards. Protect your altar using a white candle and a black crystal such as tourmaline to prevent negative energies from entering the space.

You might like to dedicate your altar to a particular intention. For example, if you are manifesting wealth and money, cover your altar in a green or gold cloth, and add coins, buttons, and other metal or coin-shaped objects.

An altar dedicated to love could be covered in a pink or red scarf, with petals, shells, and self-love affirmations. Alternatively, use your altar to develop your own unique relationship to magick. Make art about the symbols and metaphors that are significant to you, offer flowers or pretty stones as tokens of gratitude for the abundance in your life, and keep framed photos of loved ones or role models on your altar.

TAROT

Tarot is a series of 78 images printed on a deck of cards. There are certain elements that all tarot decks share—characters, card meanings, and structure, for example. Today, many artists have created their own interpretation of the tarot, so there are hundreds of decks out there—one to suit every taste.

You'll also see oracle decks available. These are less structured and without a unifying system of symbols. Oracle cards will have their own system of meaning, often with messages printed on the cards themselves.

Tarot can be used for divination to seek information about the past, present, and future. Turn to the tarot for life advice, to see challenges from a new perspective, and for self-discovery.

HOW TO READ THE TAROT

Begin by preparing your space—either with a banishing ritual, by burning incense, or meditating for a couple minutes. Clear your space and arrange any objects you want to use in your reading. It's also fine to read the cards quickly and without other objects present—just take a moment to clear your mind and calm your body.

First select a spread—turn to pages 87–89 for examples. Tap the deck three times to remove any stagnant energy, then shuffle. Focus your mind on your intentions or questions for the reading. If you're reading for someone else, tune into their energy and hold their image in your mind.

When you've finished shuffling, use your intuition to select the number of cards you need, or ask the person you're reading for to choose them.

Place the cards face down and turn them over one by one, taking in the images and noting where your eye is drawn and what meanings intuitively come to you. Check your deck's guide or the next few pages for more information on each card's meaning.

TAROT DOESN'T PREDICT THE FUTURE. TAROT FACILITATES IT.

PHILIPPE ST. GENOUX

THE MAJOR ARCANA

The major arcana is made up of 22 archetypes. Check your deck's guide for a more in-depth exploration of meaning, or here for quick interpretations:

1. Fool: new beginnings
2. Magician: manipulation
3. High priestess: wisdom
4. Empress: vitality
5. Emperor: virility
6. Hierophant: tradition
7. Lovers: union
8. Chariot: conquest
9. Strength: control
10. Hermit: secrets
11. Wheel of fortune: transformation
12. Justice: balance
13. Hanged man: different perspective
14. Death: ending and rebirth
15. Temperance: purification
16. Devil: power
17. Tower: sudden change
18. Star: hope
19. Moon: caution
20. Sun: revelation
21. Judgment: ruling
22. World: completion

THE MINOR ARCANA

The minor arcana is made up of 56 cards split into four suits. A tarot guide will give you an in-depth message for each card, here's a quick interpretation:

SUITS:

Swords—air, knowledge, words, and actions
Pentacles—earth, material possessions, money, and work
Wands—fire, energy, growth, and passion
Cups—water, emotions, creativity, and relationships

NUMBERS:

Aces: potential
2s: union, opposites
3s: growth, completion
4s: stability, manifestation
5s: conflict, change
6s: harmony, reconciliation
7s: reevaluation, knowledge
8s: achievement, advancement
9s: attainment, change
10s: completion, rest

COURT CARDS

These are usually named after members of the royal court. There are four court cards for each suit in a tarot deck. In some modern decks they'll be called different names such as mother, father, son, and daughter. In a tarot reading, they'll often represent a person related to the person having the reading.

Here's a brief guide to the meanings of each court card:

- **King:** an adult man, a father figure, someone in authority
- **Queen:** an adult woman, a mother figure, someone nurturing
- **Knight:** a young person, someone undergoing change, full of energy
- **Page:** a young child, someone younger than the querent, an immature personality

Pay attention to the features of the character on the court cards, as this can provide more context as to whom the card represents. Go with your intuition— nothing has to be overt in tarot, and metaphors are often more reliable than concrete details.

TWO-CARD SPREAD

This simple tarot spread is easy to incorporate into a morning self-care ritual. Two cards' meanings combined give each other context and depth that will give you insight into your emotional state, your choices, and how your day is likely to go.

* Simply shuffle and pull two cards from your tarot deck, laying them next to each other.
* The card on the left represents the past, and the card on the right represents the future.
* Notice what elements of the cards your eyes are drawn to.
* Notice what your intuition tells you and what thoughts or memories come up.
* Check the cards' meanings in a guide—put the two together and see what new meaning arises.
* Pay attention to the similarities and differences between the cards.
* You could leave your two cards out on your altar (see page 79) or take a photo on your phone, then take another look at them as part of your bedtime routine. How do the cards relate to your experiences during the day?

CELTIC CROSS TAROT SPREAD

This traditional tarot spread will give you deep insight. It can be performed for yourself or for someone else, and you can use a Celtic cross to explore a specific question or to take stock of your life in general.

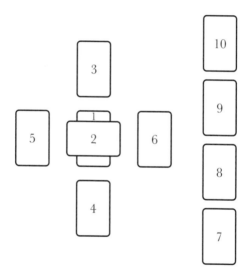

1. You/the querent

2. What's in your way

3. Wisdom from your higher self

4. Message from your subconscious

5. The past

6. The future

7. Where your power lies

8. What you need

9. Hopes and fears

10. Outcome

MANIFESTATION

Manifestation is the practice of making your thoughts reality. The universal law of attraction says that anything you can imagine can become yours. The idea of manifestation has been around for millennia—see page 77 and the ancient Aramaic translation of *abracadabra*.

Manifesting your desires requires more than just thinking about them, the key is to communicate them effectively with the universe and truly believe that they are already yours.

Many successful people credit a manifestation practice with their achievements. Oprah Winfrey, Lady Gaga, and Jim Carrey have all spoken publicly about their use of the law of attraction in realizing their dreams.

HOW TO MANIFEST YOUR DESIRES

Think of something you're aiming for or that you really want to possess. It could be a new job that pays a specific amount, a partner that ticks certain boxes, or you might want to feel more joyful, supported, or confident.

In order to manifest what you desire, close your eyes and visualize yourself already having it. For example, if you want to be a published author, you could visualize the front cover of your debut novel, sitting on the shelves of your favorite bookstore.

Imagine how it feels to be a person who has the thing you want. Concentrate hard, so you begin to feel the emotions you'll feel when you achieve your dream. Speak out loud, in the present tense, affirming that your desire is already yours. Now you've communicated your desire to the universe, you can relax in the knowledge that the universe is doing its part. It's important to take steps toward your goal too: make it as easy as possible for the universe to deliver your manifestation by putting in the work.

That's manifestation in a nutshell! There are many ways to strengthen and speed up your manifestation practice, read on for some of the best.

INTENTIONS AND AFFIRMATIONS

Without knowing it, we communicate with the universe and manifest our realities every day. The universe does not differentiate between negative and positive, it hears only your words. So if you speak more about what you *don't* want than what you do want, the theory goes that the universe will send you more of what you don't want.

However, you don't need to think of universal magick as some kind of thought police. You are communicating most strongly when you do so intentionally, and this is where the power of intention and affirmation comes into play.

Speaking in the present tense tells the universe that your desire is already yours, that you are a match for it, and that you are ready to receive it. When you say "I want . . ." the universe understands that you are in the state of wanting, not in the state of receiving.

Craft your desire into a present-tense affirmation, for example:

"I have a job that pays six figures."

Write your affirmation down, think it regularly, say it out loud to yourself.

MATCHING VIBRATIONS

To super-charge your manifestation process, the goal is to match the vibration of your desire. Take real-life steps toward being the kind of person who already possesses the thing you're manifesting—whether literal or metaphorical. Here are a few ideas:

- If you want to buy a house, make or source a house-shaped trinket.

- If you're manifesting your dream job, dress like you already have it.

- If you desire a specific amount of money, write yourself a check for that amount and keep it in your purse or wallet.

- If you're seeking a new best friend, work on being a great friend to yourself and others.

- If you wish to travel somewhere, prepare a recipe from that place and focus on your intention while you eat it.

STRATEGIES FOR AMPLIFYING MANIFESTATION

Aside from matching the vibration of your intention, there are other actions you can take to amplify your manifestations. Here are some of the most powerful:

MAKE A SIGIL

There's a guide to creating your own sigil on pages 74–75. Once you've designed one for your intention, draw it on your body, in your journal, and anywhere that's associated with your desire. For example, if you're manifesting a new intimate partner, you could draw your sigil somewhere on your bed. If you're manifesting money, keep a piece of paper with your sigil in your purse or wallet.

CRYSTALS

On pages 49–50 there's a guide to some of the most popular crystals for occult magick. But there are literally hundreds of crystals, all with their own specific meanings and powers. Research crystals associated with your intention and buy small ones to keep in your bag or pocket or on your desk.

FUTURE-SELF JOURNALING

Creating a future-self journal is a powerful way to add detail to your intentions and increase your powers of manifestation. Write in the present tense, as if you are already experiencing the things you wish to manifest. Try watching YouTube video tours of your dream vacation location, job, or home, then journal about the experience as if it were happening to you.

Try these prompts for future-self journaling—respond to them in the present tense, as if your intentions have already manifested:

- Describe your home

- Describe a typical day in your life

- What emotions do you feel every day?

- Describe the people closest to you

- Describe your relationship with money

- Describe your job

TRUSTING THE PROCESS

Once you've communicated your intention or desire to the universe, it's important to relax about the outcome. Urgency, impatience, and tension will block or delay your manifestation from entering your life, so it's a great time to focus on your emotional well-being. Read self-help books to understand any emotional blockages or patterns that might be getting in the way of receiving your desires.

A full-moon ritual is perfect for releasing any barriers between you and your intentions:

- At the full moon, sit somewhere you can see the moon and light a candle.
- Write what you want to let go of on a small piece of paper—it could be something specific or simply "all that no longer serves my highest good."
- Use the candle to carefully light the paper, then put it in a flame-proof bowl.
- Meditate on the burning paper until it has completely burned.
- Visualize yourself letting go and releasing.
- Thank the moon.

THE ENTIRE UNIVERSE IS CONSPIRING TO GIVE YOU EVERYTHING THAT YOU WANT.

ABRAHAM HICKS

SPELL CASTING

Casting occult spells in the twenty-first century requires a mix of ritual and intention. While there are traditional, prescribed methods for spell casting found in the grimoires of occult practitioners through the ages, designing and executing your own spell in a way that's unique and meaningful for you is the most potent way to practice magick in the modern world.

One rule remains eternal—the rule of three. Whatever energy you put out into the world—whether it be positive or negative—will return to you threefold. With this in mind, it isn't wise to cast spells that seek to harm others.

Casting a spell involves performing a ritual and guiding the energy produced by the ritual using an intention. On the next few pages you'll find a collection of spells for a variety of purposes. Feel free to follow them to the letter, or adapt them to better suit your practice.

MOON MAGICK

Different spells are more powerful when the moon is in different phases.

- **New moon**—set intentions

- **Waxing crescent**—money and work spells

- **First quarter**—love and luck spells

- **Waxing gibbous**—pause and reflect

- **Full moon**—clearing obstacles

- **Waning gibbous**—protection and cleansing spells

- **Last quarter**—healing and abundance spells

- **Waning crescent**—gratitude and offerings

LOVE SPELL FOR ATTRACTING YOUR DREAM PARTNER

You will need:

- Pink candle
- Rose or clear quartz
- Paper and pen
- Red string, wool, or ribbon

Method:

Clear your space using a banishing ritual or by burning incense.

Light your candle and place your crystal(s) between you and the candle.

By the light of your candle, write the characteristics you seek in a partner on the piece of paper. Be specific, and include characteristics of both personality and appearance (the latter will help you recognize them when you meet).

When you're done, roll up your list and wind the red string around it three times.

Focus on the candle flame and recite the characteristics on your list. When you finish speaking, blow out the candle and visualize your intention being released into the universe.

Keep your list somewhere safe and out of sight.

MONEY SPELL FOR INCREASING WEALTH

You will need:

- Enough money to buy a tomato
- Compost
- Small plant pot
- Paper towel

Method:

Hold the money in your hand and tap it three times with one finger to cleanse its energy.

Speak your intention to the money—it could be a specific amount of money or a purchase you wish to make.

Go to a shop and buy a tomato—go for the one (or package) that you're drawn to intuitively. Pay for the tomato using the enchanted money. It's important to use the physical money in this spell, so don't be tempted to put it on a card.

Cut the tomato in half and scoop out the seeds. Eat the rest of the tomato while visualizing your intention.

Place the seeds on a paper towel to dry out overnight.

Fill your plant pot with compost and plant the tomato seeds, covering with another thin layer of compost.

Care for your seeds by keeping the soil damp. When a seed sprouts, transfer it to its own pot. As your tomato plant grows, so will your bank balance.

PROTECTION SPELL

You will need:

- 3 white candles
- Bell (optional)
- Piece of white string, wool, or ribbon about 2m in length

Method:

Cleanse your space and light the white candles to signify the beginning of the spell.

Arrange your piece of white string in an approximate circle on the floor. Alternatively, if you have a patio or deck, you can use white chalk to draw a circle.

Sit within the circle and visualize a white light stretching upward from the circle to form a wall.

Say three times: "I am safe and protected."

If you wish to include anyone else in your protection spell, repeat this step for each person: "[name] is safe and protected."

Ring the bell and move it around the circle in a clockwise direction. If you don't have a bell, you can snap your fingers instead. The vibrations made by the sound will help the protective energy "stick" to you.

When you have completed your circle of sound, wait for the sound to come to a complete stop, then blow out the candles.

SPELL TO FIND SOMETHING LOST

You will need:

- Object to represent the lost item
- Rosemary (dried or fresh)
- Green candle

Method:

Cleanse your space and light the candle.

Place the object so it is touching the candle. Your object could be a miniature version of the lost thing, or any object that has some loose literal or metaphorical connection to what is lost. For example, you could use a piece of obsidian for a lost black cat or a penny to represent money you have lost.

Smell the rosemary and place it next to the candle.

Focus on the flame and recite these words: "What is lost is now found, intact and without harm."

Visualize the lost thing and blow out the candle.

Relax and allow the lost thing to return to you.

CORD-CUTTING SPELL TO RELEASE EMOTIONAL ATTACHMENTS

You will need:

- Length of string, wool, or ribbon
- Paper and pen
- Salt
- Water
- Bowl
- Scissors
- Black candle

Method:

Cleanse your space and light the candle.

On the piece of paper, write the name of the person or thing you wish to release.

Roll it into a scroll and wind the string around the paper three times.

Fill your bowl with water and add a tablespoon of salt.

Unwrap the paper and wind the string around two of your fingers.

Submerge the piece of paper in the water, so that the ink runs.

Using the scissors, carefully get ready to cut the string that is wound around your fingers. As you cut, recite these words: "I release the ties that bind. I claim that which is mine. And so it is."

Visualize a cord between you and the thing you are releasing and imagine it breaking, setting you free.

Blow out the candle to signify the spell's completion.

Dispose of the piece of paper by burying or recycling it somewhere away from your home.

SCRYING AND DIVINATION

There are many magickal ways of telling the future and gaining insight. In this section you'll find an introduction to some of the most popular and powerful occult divination techniques. These practices will allow you to tune in to the energies all around you, as well as recognize symbols and heed your intuition. Be prepared when gazing into the future, though, because you might not always like what you see.

MIRROR SCRYING

Mirror scrying involves gazing into a dark, blank, reflective surface and observing the visions that come from it. You can use any smooth, blank surface—a crystal ball, an obsidian disc, or even your blank phone screen—as a scrying mirror.

Once you have your scrying mirror, grab a journal and you're all set. Begin by blocking out as many distractions as possible and close your eyes. Tune into the energies around you and when you feel ready, open your eyes. Stare into the reflective surface (it's OK if you need to blink now and then) and look for patterns, symbols, and pictures. You may see moving images and even words or numbers. Thoughts or memories might pop into your head suddenly. Jot down all the things you see, think, and feel, even if they seem, on the surface, to be unrelated to the divinatory practice.

After scrying, let your visions sit with you for a while. The message may be immediately obvious, or it may begin to make sense to you over the coming days.

FIRE AND SMOKE SCRYING

Scrying with a flame or smoke can be done on a campfire, with a fire in a fireplace, or using a lit candle. First, cleanse your space, take any necessary safety precautions, and make sure you won't be disturbed.

Get your journal, light your fire or candle, and take some time just watching the flames. When you feel ready, find a part of the fire where your gaze can comfortably rest, and focus on this point.

Pay attention to the movement and shapes of the fire—do you notice any images, forms, or patterns? Take note of any thoughts or feelings that arise during scrying, as these are relevant too. Listen also to the crackling of the fire—write down any words or sounds you hear.

When you're ready to finish scrying, let your gaze rest away from the fire for a few moments. Be sure to review your notes later on, as the messages can take a while to begin making sense.

WATER SCRYING

This full moon water scrying ritual is a powerful way to harness the moon's energy in your divination practice.

You will need:

- Journal and pen
- Dark-colored bowl
- Enough water to fill the bowl

Method:

At the full moon, go outside and place your bowl on a flat surface. Cleanse the space.

Close your eyes and attune yourself to the energy around and above you.

When you're ready, open your eyes and pour the water into the bowl.

Position yourself so that you can see the moon's light reflected in the water.

Stare into the water, looking for images, words, numbers, or patterns. Make a note of these and any thoughts, memories, and feelings that come to you.

When you're ready to finish, you can leave the water out overnight to charge it with the moon's energy or pour it onto the ground as an offering.

USING A PENDULUM

Using a pendulum like the ones described on pages 62–63 is the ideal method for obtaining a "yes" or "no" answer.

Cleanse your space and clear your mind, then hold your pendulum by the end of its chain so it can swing freely, keeping your hand still. Begin by asking a question to which you know the answer is "yes," like your name or birthday. You'll see the pendulum begin to sway of its own accord—it might be in clockwise or counterclockwise circles, back and forth, or side to side. Observe its movements—this is how your pendulum will tell you "yes" during this reading.

Repeat this step with a question to which the answer is "no."

Now you are in communication with your pendulum and you can ask it questions.

A pendulum can also be used to find lost things by observing its movements over a map or using it to guide you to a specific place in your home.

CEROMANCY

Ceromancy is the practice of reading melted candle wax. Like reading tea leaves or coffee grounds, it requires a question and will provide an answer.

You will need:
- Bowl
- Water
- Candle and matches
- Journal and pen

Method:
Cleanse the space, fill the bowl with water, and light the candle.

Clear your mind and write your question in your journal.

Carefully hold the candle over the water and allow the wax to drip onto the water's surface.

After a few moments, blow out the candle and set it aside.

Gaze into the water at the shapes the wax has formed and the movements it makes in the water. Look for shapes, images, patterns, numbers, and letters. Let your intuition guide you toward meaning and interpretation.

COMMUNING WITH SPIRITS

Contacting the dead and spirits from other realms, such as angels or spirit guides, has been part of occult magick for thousands of years. Followers of the occult believe that those who have passed into another plane of existence have messages and wisdom for us to benefit from. In this section you'll find some of the occult practices used today for communicating with spirits and how you can strengthen your own abilities.

OUIJA BOARD

A Ouija board can be used alone or with others. It originated as a parlor game in the nineteenth century, so it does lend itself to practicing in company.

You'll need a table or a space on the floor and a planchette or small upturned glass to move around the board. Place your planchette in the center of the board where there is a blank space.

Say out loud an invitation to benevolent spirits. You can make up your own or find one online—it will go something like this: "I am inviting in any spirits serving my highest good."

Place your hands on the planchette and allow any spirits present to move it to different letters on the board. If you have a question, ask it out loud and wait for an answer via the planchette.

When you're ready to end, slide the planchette to "goodbye" and lift your hands from it.

USING A OUIJA BOARD SAFELY

Never practice magick or use a Ouija board under the influence of alcohol or drugs. If at any point you feel the presence of a malevolent or negative spirit, slide the planchette to "goodbye" and flip it over to release the spirit.

There have been reports of disturbing experiences with Ouija boards; if you are troubled by any magickal experience, it's a good idea to visit your doctor.

AUTOMATIC WRITING AND DRAWING

Allowing occult energies and your subconscious to take over your hand will enable you to channel messages onto paper.

To try it, clear your mind and either close your eyes or concentrate on a spot in the distance.

Take a pen or pencil and allow it to move freely over the paper, never looking at it.

When you're ready, put the pen down and take a look at the words, images, and marks you've made on the paper.

This can also be performed using a keyboard or smartphone. Divert your attention elsewhere and allow your fingers to type of their own accord.

This can be a difficult skill to master, so don't be discouraged if it takes a few tries to channel a message.

THE FOUR "CLAIRS" OF INTUITION

When we use occult magick, we are able to sense beyond the boundaries of the physical world, using the four "clairs" of intuition:

- **Clairvoyance:** seeing images
- **Clairaudience:** hearing voices
- **Clairsentience:** recognizing feelings
- **Claircognizance:** knowing

You may have experienced one or many of these phenomena already, perhaps only faintly. Strengthen your powers by paying close attention to even faint messages you intuitively pick up.

Journal about the messages to encourage more, and place crystals such as amazonite, lapis lazuli, and sodalite on your forehead or heart to amplify your psychic abilities.

Take time each day to let your intuition guide you by paying attention to which energies you're drawn to in any given setting. For example, let your intuition pick out a cake from the coffee shop or notice which exhibits you're drawn to in your local museum.

SPIRIT GUIDES

A spirit guide is a supernatural being who will protect you from negative influences and offer guidance. Spirit guides can come to us as deceased loved ones, angels, ancestors, or any other wise presence.

Invite your spirit guides in by setting an intention to connect with them and listening out for their guidance. Crystals such as celestite, leopard jasper, or scolecite carried in your pocket, held in your hand, or placed on your forehead will aid you in channeling your spirit guides. Regular intuitive rituals—such as tarot, scrying, and journaling—will strengthen your bond by deepening your communication and understanding of your guides.

Once you've connected with your spirit guide or guides, you can call on them to help you with decisions, planning, relationships, and anything else you could use some advice about!

MAKE YOURSELF SPIRIT-FRIENDLY

Getting in touch with spiritual beings and energies can be hit or miss, but it's worth persevering. Here are some tips for maximizing your chances:

LOOK OUT FOR SYNCHRONICITIES

Coincidences and *déjà vu* are messages from the universe and your spirit guides—when you see one, acknowledge it as a sign and consider what it could mean for you.

CLEANSE YOUR ENERGY

Use herbs, the light of the full moon, ritual baths with candles and crystals, and visualization to cleanse your mind, body, and home of stale and negative energy, clearing the way for benevolent spirits.

MEDITATE

Learning to clear and relax your mind helps open channels of communication.

WELCOME THEM IN

Place or mount a small token of welcome, like a crystal or shell, on or just outside your front door to signify an invitation.

CHAPTER SEVEN

JOIN A COVEN OR PRACTICE SOLO

A coven is a group of witches who gather together to perform occult magick. While a lot of magick can be practiced alone, some rituals and celebrations are best observed as part of a group. Being part of a coven is entirely optional, and in this chapter we'll explore some of the pros and cons of group magick, as well as tips and advice for becoming part of a coven.

PRACTICING ALONE

As you develop your magickal practice, your intuition and unique inner system of meaning and metaphor will grow in depth and complexity. Because of this, many choose to keep their personal practice private and solitary—it can feel difficult and vulnerable to share your gifts and insights with others.

Building an altar for your magick is especially important if you practice alone. Setting aside a space that is just for you gives your magick a sense of groundedness and manifests it in the physical world.

Whether you keep your magick just for you, or share it with others, your relationship with yourself is the most important one you'll ever have. Allow magick to nourish your emotions, bring you greater self-knowledge, and increase your self-love.

STARTING A COVEN

If you feel called to share and develop your craft with others, you can start a coven. Some believe that a coven must be made up of 13, but three like-minded people is enough to get started.

Covens can connect on social media, on video calls and online forums, as well as in real life. If you're looking for new members, use your manifestation practice to draw in your dream coven members or post an ad on social media, meetup.com, or reddit.com/r/covenfinder.

Once you have your coven, arrange a regular gathering at the new or full moon each month. Plan a loose structure for the gathering, perhaps beginning and ending with a meditation. Try picking a theme for each gathering, taking inspiration from the wheel of the year, the chakras, or signs of the zodiac.

Money is a form of energy, so if your coven has running costs don't be afraid to ask for contributions to ensure the gatherings support all members equally. Likewise, share the emotional, physical, and organizational work among the coven, giving everyone a stake in its growth.

JOINING A COVEN

If you'd like to become part of an established coven, begin with your manifestation practice. Visualize the kind of people you'd like to share and develop your craft with, consider how far you'd travel or if you'd prefer an online group.

Search social media, meetup.com, and reddit.com/r/covenfinder for a perfect coven that's open to new members.

Once you find your coven, take some time to learn about the rituals and routines of the group. If you see an opportunity for you to contribute your unique gifts—like hosting a workshop, performing a reading, or something more practical like building an online forum or sourcing a venue—offer up your ideas, allowing your energy to contribute to the coven's development.

A WORD OF WARNING

Practicing magick is a deeply nourishing act with many benefits. Whether you choose to practice alone or with others, it will bring you closer to your innate power, growing your sense of self-love and self-awareness.

Despite our occult wisdom and magickal practices, we are all human beings. Just like any group of people, a coven has the potential to fill you up or to deplete you. Stay tuned in to your intuition, energy levels, boundaries, and values, and if you find yourself as part of a coven that no longer serves you, it's OK to release yourself and follow your own best interests.

Perhaps you want to let go of a friend, a group, or even a spell you've cast—you can do so by using a simple banishing spell. This banishing spell will neutralize the energy you've put into the connection or spell, allowing it to fall away without effort.

A BANISHING SPELL

You will need:
- Cauldron or heat-proof bowl
- Water
- Black candle
- Paper and pen

Method:
Stand the candle inside your bowl or cauldron, loosen the wax at its base if needed.

Fill the cauldron or bowl with water, so the candle is about three-quarters submerged.

Write the name of the person or thing you wish to neutralize and banish from your life on the piece of paper.

Light the candle and carefully burn the piece of paper in its flame.

Allow the candle to burn down, focusing your attention on its flame. Watch as the flame is snuffed out when the wick meets the water.

FINAL WORD

The occult holds wisdom and potential you won't find anywhere else, and I hope you've enjoyed this introduction to its mysteries. As a philosophy, the occult is both ancient and modern, thanks to its ability to move with the times and remain at the boundaries of Earthly knowledge.

Take this book as a starting point in creating your own unique practice, using your strengths, curiosity, and intuition to tap into the occult magick that resonates and aligns with you. Take some time to let what you've learned sink in—pay attention to your dreams, see where your curiosity leads you, and observe what manifests in your life over the coming weeks.

In embracing your innate magick, you join a long and colorful history of occult practitioners, witches, and mediums. Use the traditions, knowledge, and rituals from the past to co-create and supercharge your unique magickal practice.

You may feel called to read more on the subject of the occult, and you'll find recommendations on the next couple of pages. In the end, no book can tell you about your own magick because it is only fully knowable to yourself. Use the occult as a tool for awakening your power and remember to practice responsibly.

YOUR VISION WILL BECOME CLEAR ONLY WHEN YOU CAN LOOK INTO YOUR OWN HEART. WHO LOOKS OUTSIDE, DREAMS; WHO LOOKS INSIDE, AWAKES.

CARL JUNG

FURTHER RESOURCES

Light Magic for Dark Times by Lisa Marie Basile and Kristen J. Sollee

The Little Book of Witchcraft by Astrid Carvel

The Little Book of Tarot by Xanna Eve Chown

The Element Encyclopedia of 500 Spells by Judika Illes

The Element Encyclopedia of Secret Signs and Symbols by Adele Nozedar

The Occult, Witchcraft and Magic: An Illustrated History by Christopher Dell

The Beginner's Guide to the Occult by Deborah Lipp

The Little Book of Symbols by Christine Barrely

The Little Book of Manifestation by Astrid Carvel

INTERNET

www.thehoodwitch.com
Everyday witchcraft, beginners' guides to everything
from crystal healing to tarot and daily horoscopes

www.biddytarot.com
Encyclopedic tarot website

www.reddit.com/r/covenfinder
International message board for connecting covens

www.whrin.org
Witchcraft and Human Rights Information Network,
a charity working for the end of persecution and
hunting of witches worldwide